The Management Guide to Running Meetings

Kate Keenan

GW00746648

Ⓞ
Oval Books

Published by Oval Books
335 Kennington Road
London SE11 4QE

Telephone: (0207) 582 7123
Fax: (0207) 582 1022
E-mail: info@ovalbooks.com

First published by Ravette Publishing.
This edition published by Oval Books.

First edition 1996
New edition 1999

Series Editor – Anne Tauté
Editor – Catriona Scott

Cover designer – Jim Wire, Quantum
Printer – Cox & Wyman Ltd

Cover – A sure sign of an effective
meeting is when the coffee goes
cold in the cups.

Acknowledgments:
Jeremy Bethell
Tony Clark
Barry Tuckwood

ISBN: 1-902825-80-2

Contents

This book is dedicated to
those who would like to manage better
but are too busy to begin.

Running Meetings

Everyone agrees that positive and productive outcomes are the key objectives of any meeting. Unfortunately, many people say that a large proportion of the meetings they attend are futile and achieve little if anything at all. Yet running meetings productively and efficiently is a relatively straightforward process. Even if you have never run one before, doing a little preparation in advance and being prepared to take control will go a long way to ensuring that the meeting achieves its purpose.

This book shows you how to run meetings and helps you to get the best out of them. It offers simple, effective ways of making certain that any meetings you run are considered by those who attend to be worthwhile.

★ ★ ★ ★ ★

1. Why Meetings Do Not Work

Managing anything usually means that meetings are required, yet the general opinion of meetings is often: "That was a complete waste of time". This is a sentiment frequently voiced by those who have participated in meetings which were badly organised and lacked control. After a meeting you may have heard people say, or even said yourself:

- "I might just as well not have been there" which implies that not everyone got a chance to contribute.

- "It had nothing to do with me" which signifies that some people felt excluded from the decisions that were made.

- "All my points were criticised" which suggests that the speaker did not get a fair hearing.

- "I didn't see much point in having a meeting" which indicates that there was no clear purpose.

- "I was only there to make up the numbers" which implies that the outcome was considered to be a foregone conclusion.

All too often meetings result in discontent because the meeting was not properly run so the people attending never had a chance to contribute.

Poor Management

For meetings to be effective they require direction. If there is no nominated individual to manage the proceedings in an orderly way, meetings can either wander aimlessly or become unruly, with no appreciable result.

If it is not appreciated that firm control is required, behaviour can rapidly deteriorate. On the other hand, if individuals running the meeting are not up to the task or simply do not understand what they should do, they may not be capable of exerting their influence in the required manner, such as:

- **Keeping to the agenda and guiding the proceedings to a conclusion** so people do not become irritated or consider the meeting unproductive.

- **Encouraging all points of view** so that each person attending has an opportunity to express an opinion and does not end up feeling excluded and resentful.

- **Controlling the discussion** so there is time for views to be considered and talk does not linger too long on one point.

- **Winding up the meeting with a proper summary** so there is a clear statement of what was achieved and what tasks people have to do as a result.

- **Recording** what was decided so there are no misunderstandings or excuses at the next meeting.

It is often the lack of direction in a meeting and the lack of opportunity to have a 'say' which causes people to conclude that many meetings are a waste of time and effort.

Lack of Structure

Meetings are often in trouble even before they begin because no-one takes the trouble to prepare an agenda listing the items to be discussed. A meeting which takes place without a clearly defined structure is likely to create more problems than it solves. For instance:

- Those who attend will not be able to prepare, so they will not have required information to hand.

- There are no time constraints so the meeting concludes when people run out of steam, get bored or have to leave.

- The same topic is gone over several times while other items are not brought up at all.

- There is uncertainty about why the meeting was called, what its purpose is, and what everyone is doing there.

If people do not know exactly what needs to be deliberated at the meeting, they will not be able to participate positively. This means discussion will veer off at various tangents so the meeting will almost certainly not achieve its objective.

Not Valuing the Meeting

The attitude people have to a meeting plays a large part in determining whether or not it will be worthwhile. Indications that the meeting is not valued include:

- Sending an uninformed substitute because the meeting is not thought to be important enough.

- Not having done what should have been done before the meeting.

- Accepting messages or receiving phone-calls during the meeting.

- Not bringing information or notes required for the meeting.

Sometimes the wrong people are at the meeting; at other times the right people fail to attend. People have even been known to turn up for the wrong meeting, and how long it takes them to realise it is the wrong meeting (if at all) will depend on how well the meeting is being run and controlled.

To achieve productive results, it is important that the right people attend the meeting in the right frame of mind.

Difficult Conditions

People find it difficult to make an intelligent contribution if the venue for the meeting is not comfortable, and poor conditions can end up being the focus of attention. It is as difficult to concentrate when discussion continues for too long without a break, as it is when there are constant interruptions or when people talk amongst themselves. All these things mean the issues will not be given undivided attention, and the net result is that the meeting ends up being less constructive than it should be.

No Need for the Meeting

A meeting takes time and effort yet people often call one simply because they have not thought through suitable alternatives which could provide the same results. Getting people together can provide a certain 'comfort' factor, a familiar way of doing things, so it goes on happening even when it may be unnecessary.

Meetings are also used as a way to delay making decisions or to avoid taking personal responsibility. It is always useful to take a step back and question what the meeting is for, or even whether it is needed at all.

Summary: Usefulness of Meetings

Meetings are a means to an end; they are rarely an end in themselves. The conclusion of a meeting is usually just the beginning for other activities, even if it is simply the setting up of another meeting.

By regarding meetings as a constructive way of making decisions, you will find it much easier to direct your efforts. This means that the purpose for which the meeting was called is more likely to be achieved.

Questions to Ask Yourself

Think about your attitude to meetings and answer the following questions:

✓ Have I ever thought, "That meeting was a waste of time"?

✓ Do I ever feel despondent at the prospect of attending a meeting?

✓ Have I ever attended chaotic meetings?

✓ Have I ever been at a meeting where I was not clear about my reason for being there?

✓ Have I ever gone to a meeting and not given it my full attention?

✓ Do I feel that some meetings I attend could be better organised?

✓ Do I ever wonder why a meeting has been called?

If you have answered 'Yes' to several or most of these questions, you may need to give some attention to what you need to do when *you* run meetings.

You Will Be Doing Better If...

★ You recognise why some meetings do not achieve results.

★ You realise that your attitude towards a meeting can contribute to its success.

★ You appreciate that meetings need to be managed properly.

★ You know that if people are not comfortable, they will not concentrate.

★ You understand that people need to know what will be discussed at the meeting.

★ You are clear about the objectives of the meetings you run.

★ You are certain that any meeting you initiate is really needed.

2. Understanding What Happens at Meetings

Meetings have a momentum of their own and will vary in pace, rhythm and mood. But because they are bringing people together as a group, they also exert another influence – one which imposes a predictable pattern of behaviour on the participants.

So before they can achieve anything of value, the group has to learn to work together effectively – a process which takes four separate stages:

1. **Forming: the settling-in stage**

   In this opening period people get their bearings and try to get the measure of each other in a polite way (since they have not yet found a reason to be rude to each other). They seek to know one another's attitudes and backgrounds and want to establish the ground rules.

2. **Storming: the boxing and coxing stage**

   Once people are more comfortable, they will start to open up. They may indulge in minor verbal skirmishes which can lead to the meeting becoming disorganised and difficult to control. This is where people challenge each other and test their impressions, re-assessing them if necessary.

3. **Norming: the working productively stage**
As meetings progress, ideas are developed and compromises reached, which involve alliances being made and deals being struck in order to get things moving forward. A framework is clearly established which enables everyone present to know what is expected of them.

4. **Performing: the producing results stage**
At this final stage people produce consensus and obtain results because they want to bring the meeting to a conclusion. Performance will now take precedence over everything else.

It is only in the last phase that meetings can produce efficient and effective results. Should decisions be made in either of the two middle phases, they are often half-baked and lacking in precision.

Meetings may operate at half power because people fail to work through some of the issues in the earlier stages. For example, some may be pulling in different directions because they have not yet learned to co-operate or to appreciate each other's contributions. Others might be using the meeting to achieve their personal and unstated aims – they may have hidden agendas.

How long each phase lasts depends on the people present and how well they know each other, but understanding this sequence of events makes it easier to manage the pace of the meeting and prevent things from getting stuck for too long in a particular phase.

Group Dynamics

When decisions are made by a group of people, they are often substantially different from those they would have made if they had been on their own. This is because a form of herd instinct comes into play which makes people go along with the prevailing pressures. It affects both the debate before decisions are made and the decisions themselves.

Group Pressure in Debate

In groups, people fear making fools of themselves. They become self-conscious about what they think, and often begin to doubt their own judgement. This pressure can have various effects. For instance:

- People who express doubts or question the validity of majority views are pressurised into accepting the group consensus.

- People who take a stand feel they will lose face if they concede – no matter how much evidence there is that they are wrong.

- People who may not be able to express their views adequately can end up agreeing by default.

- People who have doubts or differ in their views may keep silent to avoid being seen to deviate from the group.

An apparent absence of objections may create an illusion of unanimity, yet this may not in fact represent the personal views which individuals hold.

Group Pressure in Decision

In groups, people take decisions which exaggerate the initial positions of individual members. This is known as 'the risky shift' and means that individual views within the group become more extreme or more cautious as the meeting goes on. More often than not, group pressure causes a shift towards greater risk.

The type of shift generally depends on the dominant individual attitudes – ones which tend to have been formed well before the meeting takes place. Riskier decisions may also be taken because individuals at the meeting tend to be freed from personal accountability since no one person can be held wholly responsible for what is decided.

If the person running the meeting declares at the outset "We ought to do 'X' ", the chances are that this is what will be agreed. As the whole purpose of most meetings is to discuss and exchange ideas, the polarising of entrenched views is counter-productive and can lead the group into making riskier decisions than are warranted.

Thus, if groups are to prove less vulnerable to these pressures and if they are to perform productively, it is vital that the person running the meeting remains impartial, encourages everyone to contribute, discusses every proposition and avoids expressing personal preferences.

Summary: Group Forces

To make a meeting really productive it is necessary to take account of what is going on below the surface. When a group of people meet they need to learn how to work together and they have to go through a process of forming, storming, norming, and ultimately, performing, in order to become a coherent group.

Group pressure is brought to bear on individual thinking and decision-making which can alter the dynamics of the meeting and sometimes lead to more risky outcomes than expected.

When called upon to run a meeting, being aware of how groups develop and function makes it considerably easier to understand the forces at play.

Questions to Ask Yourself

Think about what can happen at meetings and answer the following questions:

✓ Do I appreciate that meetings go through a number of stages in order to become fully productive?

✓ Am I aware of the extent to which people are affected by being in a group?

✓ Do I recognise that people may not proffer their real views because they are worried about what others will think?

✓ Do I understand that people may not change their minds, even when they wish to do so, for fear of losing face?

✓ Do I realise that silence does not necessarily mean agreement?

✓ Am I aware that people in groups can make far riskier decisions than if they are asked to decide on their own?

You Will Be Doing Better If...

★ You appreciate that there are four distinct stages to meetings and that only the final one can produce effective results.

★ You understand that individual thinking and behaviour can be affected by the group.

★ You know that individuals can be pressurised into accepting group consensus.

★ You are aware that some people cling to their opinions because they do not want to be seen to change their minds.

★ You understand that a lack of dissent does not mean that there is consent.

★ You appreciate that people in groups make riskier decisions than they would as individuals.

★ You realise that an awareness of group dynamics is valuable when running meetings.

3.   Organising a Meeting

The amount of care given to organising a meeting contributes greatly to its success. There are several key things that you need to determine: what kind of meeting it is, what it is about, who needs to be present, and where and when it is held.

What Kind of Meeting

Meetings, like dinner parties, can be formal or informal. It is best to know which type you are organising if things are to run smoothly.

Formal Meetings

A formal meeting may be determined by its legal status or because the format has been laid down by certain rules and regulations. It usually requires a certain number of attendees. Whatever its purpose, the points of procedure involve:

- The Agenda – what is to be discussed.
- Reports and recommendations – what has been done since the last meeting.
- Motions – what action is proposed.
- Amendments – what modifications need to be made to a proposal.

- Debate – the general discussion.
- Elections and voting – the acceptance or rejection of the motions.
- Minutes – the written record of the event.
- Any other business – the issues which did not appear on the agenda.

It will be necessary to acquaint yourself with the rules (or so-called standing orders) which apply to a formal meeting or you will not be able to run it properly, and the decisions made may not be considered valid.

Informal Meetings

Informal meetings are much less constrained, but this does not mean they should be less structured. As a minimum, they should have:

- A list of topics to be discussed.
- A person responsible for running the meeting, even when it is the sort where jackets are discarded and feet put on tables.
- A record of what is decided and who will be doing what as a result.

Informal meetings may be more relaxed in the way they are run and how people behave, but there is still a need to ensure that the proceedings are well-organised and therefore productive.

What Has to be Discussed

Every meeting should have some form of agenda. You need to appreciate that this is not a perfunctory piece of paper traditionally handed round before meetings like a free leaflet in the high street. It is a working document which acts as a compass to keep everyone on a specific course. Its purpose is to prevent the least important item taking up the most time.

The sequence of the ideal agenda would look something like this:

- Purpose, date, time and place of meeting.
- Names of people attending.
- Routine topics for discussion.
- More difficult or controversial items.
- Any other business.
- The date of the next meeting.

The agenda determines the shape of the meeting. It needs to be constructed in such a way that it starts with the more straightforward areas for discussion and leads to the more difficult and usually critical aspects during the central part of the meeting. Starting with uncontentious issues, people become involved from the start. It also means that once people have said "yes", they are more inclined to say "yes" later on.

A helpful agenda is one which lets people know why the items are on the list by indicating what needs to be decided. This is not to be confused with deciding the outcome beforehand.

Sending out the agenda (even in draft form) prior to the meeting will give everyone an opportunity to prepare, and even to suggest additional items for discussion. It also gives you a chance to ask those attending to indicate if they intend to come themselves or send someone else on their behalf.

Who Attends the Meeting

When convening meetings a good maxim to remember is 'Less is more'. Two or three people frequently produce better results than a gathering of ten or twelve. The more people attending the meeting, the more control and management are required.

Should larger numbers of people be necessary, it is worth considering whether they need to be at the meeting the entire time, or whether they could arrive, make their contribution and leave again.

Who should attend the meeting will be determined by their requirement to:

- Make decisions and implement what has been agreed.
- Gather relevant information during the course of the meeting.

- Provide specific information.
- Influence the process of the meeting by providing necessary expertise or at least peace-keeping skills.

Meetings are only as good as the people who attend them. If the wrong people are present, or key people are absent, it is unlikely that effective decisions can be made. Whether people attend themselves or send a properly delegated proxy, it is essential to check that everybody who comes to the meeting has a reason and a purpose for being there.

Where the Meeting is Held

If only two or three are meeting, the venue can be quite relaxed and informal; a hotel lobby, a cubby-hole, or even a golf course. But if more than three people have a meeting, it requires proper facilities, such as adequate heat, light, air, coffee/tea/water, no distractions, and at least the same number of chairs as there are people.

The two most important things, and ones which are often forgotten, are that:

- Everyone needs to be able to see everyone else.
- The person running the meeting needs to be positioned so that eye contact is possible with everybody present.

Where people sit is also worth considering if you want to ensure that the meeting is productive. For example:

- If people are not comfortable and cannot see each other or any visual aids, charts, etc., they are unlikely to remain interested or attentive and will tend to sit doodling or day-dreaming from start to finish.

- If there are two people who are known to be argumentative characters, or who are known to take issue with each other, you need to make sure they do not sit beside, or directly opposite, each other.

- If you can place a belligerent individual next to a non-combatant, you will find that he or she is likely to be far less influential than if allowed to congregate with like minds at one end of the table.

To ensure that people sit where you want them to, a seating plan and stand-up place cards can be prepared in advance. People's names should be written on both sides of the cards so that the names face both inwards and outwards. (While those seated know who they are, the others may not, particularly the person running the meeting.)

Planning the Time

It is a good idea when considering the agenda to divide the time allocated for the meeting between the items, and keep a running total as the meeting progresses: 'Item 1. – 10 mins.[10.10]; Item 2. – 15 mins [10.25]; Item 3. – 20 mins [10.45]'. This can always be amended as you go, but it allows you to move things along, and gives you a better chance of winding up the proceedings on time.

Summary: Meeting Successfully

It is said that over 80% of a meeting's success is determined before it takes place. Having an agenda is an essential constituent since it ensures people know in advance what the meeting is about.

Giving thought to who should attend also contributes considerably to the meeting's success. With the right people there, it is easier to get things agreed.

Providing comfortable conditions concentrates everyone's minds on the subject matter, and apportioning time to each topic means that a plan exists to provide a framework for results.

Questions to Ask Yourself

Think about organising a meeting and ask yourself the following questions:

✓ Am I aware that running formal meetings requires me to follow predetermined rules?

✓ Do I appreciate that informal meetings still require a degree of formality?

✓ Do I understand the need for an agenda?

✓ Do I confirm that the purpose of each meeting is clearly stated?

✓ Do I make sure the right people are invited to the meeting, and that they know why and when their presence is required?

✓ Do I arrange for meetings to be held in reasonably comfortable surroundings?

✓ Do I make certain that the layout of the meeting is such that everybody present can see everyone else?

✓ Do I set time limits on items for discussion?

You Will Be Doing Better If...

★ You know the rules which apply to any formal meeting that you organise.

★ You appreciate that informal meetings also need to be organised with some formality.

★ You make certain that the agenda of the meeting is sent out in advance.

★ You make sure that the right people attend.

★ You ensure that the people attending know who the others are, and that everyone can see each other.

★ You set time limits to each agenda item.

4.   Controlling a Meeting

When it falls on you to run a meeting, there are several basic procedures to follow that will ensure that you conduct it effectively. By opening the meeting positively and emphasizing the time constraints, you help people to focus their attention on the purpose of the meeting. By directing the discussion and handling any disorderly conduct you keep the meeting moving forward. Then by crystallising agreement and summarising the action, you conclude the proceedings successfully.

Opening the Meeting

Once people have assembled, there are some important initial disciplines to observe:

1. **Greeting**. Meetings which are started with a welcome being given to everyone start off on a crisp note. If there are strangers present, consider asking everyone to introduce themselves in turn, stating their name and title, before you introduce the first agenda item. If someone is to arrive late, or has to leave early, now is the time to say so, to reduce the effects of later disturbance.

2. **Accepting the Minutes**. If the meeting has reconvened, or is a standing committee, it is normal to

accept the minutes or record of decisions taken at the last meeting. Only in the most formal meetings will it be necessary to read out the previous minutes. And even then, it is far easier to ask "Does anyone have a problem with page 1?" (Pause.) "Page 2?" And so on. Discourage people from nit-picking over incorrect spelling or grammar unless it concerns the actual sense of the record.

Keeping to Time

Time-keeping is a major factor in meetings. From the moment everyone sits down, you need to keep a strict eye on the time and prevent it from being wasted. Some tried and tested methods for this are:

- Start on time, even if some people have not yet arrived.

- Inform people of the amount it is costing to meet (having previously estimated how much each person present is earning and calculated what this means in terms of time). "It's costing us a total of £900 to meet for one hour. This means £15 a minute, so I suggest we make the best possible use of our time."

- Place an alarm clock in full view, stating that it is set to go off ten minutes before the due end of the meeting, so that you have time to summarise.

- Have short breaks, if it is a long meeting, to allow people to let off steam.

- Give people deadlines during the meeting to come up with ideas or suggestions. "I'd like us all to have a coffee break now and reconvene in ten minutes with a suggestion about this."

- Finish on time, or sooner, if business is concluded relatively easily.

It is important that everyone is made aware of the urgency of the meeting so that time will not be squandered, and each feels that the person running the meeting is in complete command of the schedule.

Focusing Attention

At the start, it is prudent to remind people what the meeting is to be about. This way you get them to focus their attention on what is going to be discussed. You do this by:

- Stating the existing situation or problem clearly. "The situation is that we are rather overcrowded in the office."

- Reminding people of the purpose of meeting. "The

purpose of this meeting is to find a way to re-organise the available space."

- Introducing the specific topic or topics to be discussed. "Item 1 on your agenda concerns the location of the reference books to which we all need access, and which are presently shelved behind the photocopying machine."

This stops people's attention from wandering, and focuses it on the points where decisions are required.

Directing the Discussion

Once the meeting is under way, your principal function is to direct the discussion and prevent it departing from its aim. You do this by:

- **Sticking to the Agenda**. Unless it has been agreed that the order can be changed, you need to state clearly which item on the agenda is about to be discussed. "The next item is Item 4."

- **Guiding the meeting back to its objectives**. If the meeting goes off course, it is vital you bring it back to its aims and direct peoples' energies to the business in hand. "Can we remind ourselves what we are here for?" "I don't think we want to get drawn into that issue…"

Directing the discussion also means getting the best from those present by making sure that everyone plays his or her part and takes an interest in the proceedings. This includes:

- **Noticing signs of withdrawal**. Noticing when someone is staring vacantly into space, or has not spoken for quite a while, and asking for an opinion will force the person to join in. "Jim, have you anything to add to that?" or "Jane, what do you think of that suggestion?"

- **Using expertise**. Using the expertise of the people present helps others to make informed decisions. "Fred, you were in charge of a similar situation. What was your experience when…?"

- **Making suggestions**. Proposing ideas which contain possible courses of action encourages people to think creatively and helps to keep up the pace. "Would it be a good idea to…?" "Shall we discuss the possibility of…?"

- **Supporting views**. Endorsing other people's views and ideas or stating that you think them constructive makes the discussion more productive. "That could work really well." or "Peter's idea sounds most promising. What do others think? Paul, let's start with you."

Handling Disorderly Conduct

Meetings do not always advance in an orderly manner. Occasionally the conduct of individuals can impede progress and acrimonious exchanges can lead to head-to-head clashes. Handling such conduct is stressful, but the role of the chairperson demands that you take command, however much you may dislike giving orders.

To take appropriate corrective action, you need to:

- State clearly that personal attacks are unacceptable. "Personal comments have no place in this meeting. Can we get back to the point, which is...."

- Counteract disagreement by asking for constructive suggestions. "Ted, if you don't agree with Bob, what do you suggest to solve this problem?"

- Move things forward if opinions become argumentative. "I appreciate there are strong feelings about this, but we need to move on. Perhaps the issue might be resolved by calling for a show of hands?"

Reminding people of the meeting's objectives or making an appropriate light-hearted comment can also lower the temperature should things become fraught, and bring the meeting back to an even keel. "Obviously, this is a subject that's close to your heart. Let's just take a few minutes to recap."

Disorderly conduct is rare, but thinking about how you would handle it, makes it easier to do so should the need arise.

Coping With Diversions

People in meetings cannot help creating diversions, happily straying off-course or going round and round, like a record stuck in a groove. While this is far less stressful to cope with than disorderly conduct, it is far more exasperating.

This is where tact and diplomacy are required to get the meeting back on track and keep it moving forward. To do so you have to recognise and cope with favourite forms of diversionary tactics, such as:

- **Raising difficulties**. Discussing problems and pitfalls is meat and drink to some: "We can't do that because…" "That was tried last time and it didn't work." Asking for pertinent reasons forces people to become specific in their objections and stops them from involving others in endless argy-bargy.

- **Having bees in bonnets**. Some people will use any ruse to bring up their own obsession. Letting them have their say once, and then reminding them that they have already had their say on an earlier occasion, stops them repeating themselves.

- **Going off at a tangent**. Diverting the discussion into areas which are totally irrelevant is something some people do without realising it: "Has anybody seen Volume II of the Oxford English Dictionary?" – when the meeting is about where the books are to be located. Pointing out that this is not part of the topic under discussion prevents people from getting sidetracked and brings the meeting back on course.

Crystallising Agreement

As the meeting progresses, you need to move things forward and crystallise the discussion so that the meeting can come to a consensus. You can make sure that a conclusion is reached by:

- **Presenting points of agreement and disagreement**. Identifying where people agree and highlighting where they disagree pinpoints those things which still have to be agreed. "So we all agree about…, but we still have to resolve…"

- **Asking questions**. Checking your understanding by asking questions not only ensures that you know exactly what's what but also clarifies other people's grasp of certain issues when they may not have been bold enough to ask. "Do you mean that…?" "Just let me check that I have understood…"

- **Stating intermediate conclusions.** Rounding up points as they are dealt with provides a résumé of the proceedings so far and makes people feel that, even before the end of the meeting, it is producing results. "Let's just run through what we've agreed. For Item 2, everyone considers that the best course to take will be... "

- **Making sure that there is general acceptance.** Monitoring agreement lets you forge ahead to the next point. "Can I just check that we're all happy with this decision?" "Has anyone anything further to add on this item before we move on?" "Is everyone agreed?"

This allows you to keep track of how people are thinking and act as a referee if required. It also enables decisions to accrue, so that it is easier to reach a final result.

As things are agreed, it is prudent to record them at the time. This prevents you having to go over various points at a later stage and possibly finding that someone has had a change of heart, or was never in favour of a particular decision in the first place. If you do not make sure that people fully concur with what has been agreed at the time it was agreed, the issue could be resurrected and disrupt another part of this meeting – or even the next one.

Summarising for Action

At the end of the meeting, it is essential to ensure that everyone is committed to the decisions taken. If action is to follow, there must be an overall reminder of what has been agreed. You do this by:

- **Summarising and stating conclusions clearly**. This leaves people in no doubt about what has been decided and they cannot later claim they were unaware of what was agreed. "I am now going to summarise this meeting. We met to discuss the problem of space in the office. What has been decided is as follows. Firstly, we decided … Finally, we decided that the best place for the reference books would be the reception area."

- **Fixing tasks and time limits.** This leaves no doubt as to who will do what and by what date. "It was agreed that Jim will organise … by the 30th May and liaise with Jill, who is going to…"

A good way to ensure that people do what they are supposed to do is to make a point of handing out sheets of brightly-coloured paper before you summarise and saying, "This is to jot down what you have to do before the next meeting. It's a strong colour so you'll have less likelihood of losing it".

The summary is crucial. If the action which has

been agreed is not clearly stated, very little will happen and all the effort may be wasted. A properly run meeting is one where people feel that things have been decided. They are confident that they know what to do and that something will definitely happen.

Summary: Keeping Control

Whatever form meetings take and whatever their purpose, it is up to the person running them to be clear about what needs to be achieved and to keep that aim in view. The role is not unlike that of a sheep dog, having to herd its flock into a pen. The sheep may try to stray, but constant checking and chivvying keeps them moving in the right direction.

It is also vital to sum up the contents so that action results.

Questions to Ask Yourself

Think about how you run meetings and answer the following questions:

✓ Do I open the meeting in a positive way?

✓ Do I make sure that meetings always start on time?

✓ Do I remind people what the meeting is about?

✓ Do I stick to the agenda and guide people back to it when things stray off course?

✓ Do I keep order gently but firmly?

✓ Do I let everyone have their say?

✓ Do I make sure that everyone agrees with what has been agreed at the time it is agreed?

✓ Do I summarise the conclusions and make sure everyone knows who is doing what?

You Will Be Doing Better If...

★ You appreciate that meetings need directing if they are to produce results.

★ You start your meetings on time, even if somebody has not yet turned up.

★ You work through the agenda systematically and cover all items.

★ You let everyone have their say, within limits.

★ You stop argument from escalating.

★ You bring the discussion back on track.

★ You make sure that everyone is in agreement with the decisions made at the time they are made.

★ You summarise the outcomes and indicate who is responsible for further action and by what time.

★ You focus on ensuring that the meeting produces results.

5.   Documenting a Meeting

A meeting needs to be documented so that you know precisely what was agreed and who is committed to doing what. If you are wise, you should also try to gauge opinion about how the meeting went, so you can improve the way you run the next one or make sure that you repeat your own approved performance.

Recording a Meeting

It is neither practical nor desirable for the person running the meeting to record the proceedings as well and, in certain instances, it requires a professional secretary or rapporteur. Concentrating on controlling the discussion is a full-time job, so it is best if someone else is assigned to record the meeting's progress and its outcome. When choosing someone to do this, you need bear in mind what is expected from the role.

During the Meeting

During the meeting, the job requires someone to:

- Note key points from the discussion against each agenda item, i.e. what was agreed and who will do it.

- Advise on procedure (especially for formal meetings) by knowing the conventions.

- Have previous records to hand, along with the agenda, as well as spares for those who turn up without them.

- Keep an eye on the time allocated for each item. It helps if a subtle method of communicating time constraints can be agreed before the meeting begins.

There is seldom a requirement for a verbatim record so, when making notes, the trick is to reach a balance between recording everything that is said and jotting down the odd note.

This means ensuring that the person recording the meeting knows that the task is to listen carefully to what is said, and to note only the basic details and key phrases together with the initials of the speaker in order to attribute the right things to the right people.

After the Meeting

Once the meeting is concluded, the notes taken have to be typewritten to form a record. It is wise to see that this done as soon as possible while events are still fresh in the mind. (Making it up is not an option.)

The record should contain the following:

- A heading indicating what the meeting was about and the date it was held.

- A list of the people present.
- Apologies from those who did not attend.
- A précis of what was decided about each agenda item, and who made which significant contribution.
- A summary of who will do what.

Writing the record requires the proceedings of the meeting to be presented briefly in an objective and business-like style. This is done by:

- Using reported speech, i.e. writing in the past tense, 'Jim Smith pointed out that...' 'Jane Brown said this was not a problem because...' 'It was decided...'

- Describing facts only, not giving personal opinions about what happened.

- Indicating any action to be taken by using bold type or having a separate column where appropriate action is listed beside the initials or job titles.

Before the minutes are finally issued you need to check that the account is authentic. It makes a nonsense of the whole event if inaccurate reporting leads to subsequent misunderstandings.

It helps to keep in mind that the record is not an end in itself; it acts as a spur to action. Whatever form it takes, its sole purpose is to ensure that people have no excuse not to know what went on or what they have agreed to do.

Evaluating the Meeting

It is rare for a meeting to be evaluated. Most people who run meetings are only too grateful that it is all over and that they got through it unscathed. However, if you find yourself running meetings regularly, it is helpful to know how you are doing and to assess whether others think that you are achieving results.

A simple way of doing this is to ask those attending to fill in a short, pre-prepared form before they leave, one that only takes a minute or so to complete.

The sort of things that it might ask are:

- Was this meeting of use to you?   Yes/No

- Did you manage to say all you needed to?   Yes/No

- Were you satisfied with how the meeting was run?
                                                                          Yes/No

- Do you know what you are going to do as a result of this meeting?   Yes/No

- Do you have any other comments?

Getting answers to these questions (even if no-one has the time to write anything under 'any other comments'), enables you to evaluate how well you have run the meeting and, if necessary, do better next time.

Summary: Having Evidence

Recording the proceedings is a key activity. Without written evidence it can only be recalled by hearsay and memory, neither of which is reliable.

The record needs to be succinct and should be written sooner rather than later. It should be viewed as a prompt to all those attending to act on the results of the decisions made. Therefore the bolder and clearer the record, the more likely others are to take note of what they are supposed to do, and the more likely it is that the meetings you run will result in action.

Questions to Ask Yourself

Think about how you organised the recording of the meeting and answer the following questions:

✓ Did I work productively with the person recording the meeting?

✓ Were all the key points of discussion noted and attributed?

✓ Were all decisions recorded?

✓ Was the record written up as soon after the meeting as possible?

✓ Did I make sure only facts were reported, and not personal opinions?

✓ Did I check the final version of the minutes before they were issued?

✓ Do I think the record is an accurate account of what happened at the meeting?

You Will Be Doing Better If...

★ You are supported by the person recording the meeting.

★ You find that the minutes give a succinct and objective account of the meeting.

★ You find that all decisions have been recorded.

★ You find that action to be taken by everyone attending the meeting is clearly identified.

★ You check the accuracy of the record while events are fresh in your mind.

★ You consider that the record accurately reflects the proceedings.

6. Your Attitude to Meetings

For meetings to be productive, not only do you have to be skilled at running them, you also require a positive attitude. By playing your part, taking charge, meeting expectations and doing what is assigned to you, you ensure that you get the best out of meetings and this behaviour reinforces your attitude.

Taking Charge

You have it in your power to make a meeting effective, but to do this, you need to be prepared to take charge. If you do not, you should not expect much to come of the meeting. You take charge by:

- Giving yourself permission to impose your will on others, even if it means laying down the law.

- Reminding yourself that your role gives you the authority to control the meeting.

- Convincing yourself that you can do it and are going to enjoy it.

People attending the meeting will look to you for a lead and expect you to take charge of the proceedings. Since they cannot do so themselves, you will be jeopardising the meeting if you do not.

Expecting the Best

If you have high expectations of the meeting, it is very likely to achieve results. You need to translate these expectations into practical terms by taking the positive attitude that:

- **The meeting is important**. If you do not think this, then you probably should not be running it.

- **The people attending it are necessary**. If you do not believe that everyone present needs to be there, you will find it difficult to give credence to their ideas and suggestions.

- **The time will be well spent**. If you do not think you are spending your time profitably, you will communicate this very clearly by your behaviour.

- **Good will come of it**. If you do not anticipate good results from the meeting, you will have programmed yourself to accept that nothing will come of it, and the odds are that nothing will.

The attitude you bring with you on arrival at a meeting establishes the tone at the outset. If you instantly unload your pressure on others ("It couldn't be a worse time for this meeting"), it will not only depress everyone within earshot, but unleash other expressions of despondency. But if you look optimistic and make a few good-humoured and interested comments as people are settling down, the meeting will have a better chance of starting (and thus continuing) in a positive spirit.

Taking Action

It is the sum total of the collective effort that determines the success of the meeting. If you do not carry out the tasks assigned to you, and others opt out as well, nothing will be achieved. To make sure something happens after the meeting, you need to:

- Read the minutes to verify what you are required to do and to note what others will be doing.

- Work out how to get things done by the agreed timescale, delegating what you can.

- Take action, rather than hope that you will be released from your responsibilities.

Putting things in hand while the impetus of the meeting is still with you almost guarantees that you will get them done. It also prevents you from being tempted to sidle out of your obligations. If you do your bit and others do so too, then the meeting will have been an unqualified success.

Summary: Being Productive

The attitude you take to the meetings you run will do a lot to determine whether they will be productive or not. There is little point running a meeting if you do not intend it to achieve anything. This is just a waste of everyone's time and energy. The more you expect meetings to achieve, the more productive you will find them and the more you will be rewarded.

If you are seen to be totally focused on getting results, others will take their cue from you and, if everyone gives the meeting their full attention, a successful outcome is more or less guaranteed. At the very least, you should never hear others complain about any meeting you have run being a waste of time.

Questions to Ask Yourself

Think about your attitude to any meeting you run and answer the following questions:

✓ Do I expect the meeting to achieve results?

✓ Do I communicate my positive attitude to others?

✓ Do I believe the meeting is worthwhile?

✓ Do I have confidence in my ability to run a meeting efficiently?

✓ Do I take charge?

✓ Do I lay down the law when this is called for?

✓ Do I do what I am supposed to do after the meeting?

You Will Be Doing Better If...

★ You have high expectations of the meeting.

★ You communicate a positive attitude to others.

★ You consider every meeting you run to be important and worth your time.

★ You believe in your ability to make the meeting effective.

★ You take charge of the meeting from the outset.

★ You exert your authority.

★ You anticipate good results.

★ You read and act upon the minutes immediately after the meeting.

Check List for Meetings

If you are finding that meetings are proving to be less productive than they should be, consider whether this could be because you have failed to take account of one or more of the following aspects:

Understanding Meetings

If you find it difficult to understand why people behave as they do when you are running meetings, perhaps you have not appreciated the predictable phases that groups experience before they become productive. Or perhaps you have not given proper consideration to the pressure placed on individuals by group influence which makes them behave very differently from the way they would on their own.

Organising Meetings

If the meeting does not begin on time, the items for discussion are carried out in no particular order, no-one is designated to run or record the proceedings, and the coffee never arrives, it is clearly a lack of organisation that is causing the problem. Without an agenda sent out in good time to allow people to come fully prepared, you cannot expect the meeting to produce results.

Controlling Meetings

If meetings seem to overrun the allotted time, discussion is unresolved before the next item is reached, and nobody is clear about how a decision was arrived at or what bearing it has on their actions, you may not have exerted proper control. Perhaps you are not keeping control of the conversation and have allowed it to stray too far from its aims. Possibly you are not making sure that points are clarified and agreed as you go along. Or it could be that you are not leaving yourself time to summarise who should do what at the end.

Documenting Meetings

If the record of the meeting is not all it should be, it may be that you did not explain what you required of the minutes so there is too much padding, or perhaps the presentation is poor. Or may be it does not contain all the salient facts because it was compiled too long after the event.

Your Attitude to Meetings

If you regard running a meeting as a chore and do not expect it to achieve a great deal, you can hardly be surprised if it does not. You need to be convinced that the attitude of the person running it can make the difference between failure and success.

The Benefits of Good Meetings

Meetings are an integral part of managing but it is important to bear in mind that to have results, they need to be well run, and to run them well, you need to know what needs to be done and have confidence in doing it.

The benefits of good meetings are that:

- People are better informed.

- People have a forum to express their views.

- People can explore and assess ideas.

- Agreement is reached.

- Decisions are made, even if they are decisions to take no decision.

- People are more likely to accept the decisions because they have been part of the decision-making process.

- Action is taken.

- Things get done.

Getting people involved in what is happening is a good way to gain their commitment to taking action. Running meetings effectively is the process which prompts this to happen.

Glossary

Here are some definitions in relation to Running Meetings.

Agenda – A list of items to be discussed or business to be transacted, preferably in the best possible order to achieve the objectives. From the Latin plural of agendum, meaning 'things to be done'.

Chairperson/man/woman, or just **Chair** – The person running the meeting; vital, with or without the title.

Controlling – Regulating the tempo and temperature of the meeting in order to produce results.

Disruption – Anything that interrupts the rhythm of the meeting from battery alarm bleeps to a full-scale row.

Diversion – Anything that people would rather talk about than the main issue, and which has to be curbed at all costs.

Group – A number of people considered as a collective unit; rather more than the sum total of individuals comprising it.

Individual – One whose behaviour and/or attitude can make or break the meeting.

Item – Subject for discussion or consideration.

Meeting – A means to an end.

Minutes – Official record of the proceedings.

Motion – A formal proposal, without the ring or the roses.

Preparation – A state of readiness.

Points of Procedure – The rules and regulations of formal meetings, a.k.a. standing orders.

Purpose – The whole reason for the meeting.

Quorum – The minimum number of members required in order to transact business in formal meetings.

Report – A detailed account or statement.

Result – The outcome, which, if not constructive, merely consists of fixing another meeting.

Secretary/Rapporteur – A designated professional recorder of the minutes who should need no telling how to take them.

Summary – Brief synopsis of the main points to remind people what they decided.

Time – (a) The interval between the beginning and the end; (b) the limit within which people need to complete their tasks. Neither is ever enough.

Venue – Any place for a meeting to be held which has heat, air and light bulbs that work.

Views – Other people's opinions, very few of which seem to concur.

The Author

Kate Keenan is a Chartered Occupational Psychologist with degrees in affiliated subjects (B.Sc., M.Phil.) and a number of qualifications in others.

She founded Keenan Research, an industrial psychology consultancy, in 1978. The work of the consultancy is fundamentally concerned with helping people to achieve their potential and make a better job of their management.

By devising work programmes for companies she enables them to target and remedy their managerial problems – from personnel selection and individual assessment to team building and attitude surveys. She believes in giving priority to training the managers to institute their own programmes, so that their company resources are developed and expanded.

She enjoys attending meetings but confesses to a certain degree of trepidation when running them. She finds that by forcing herself to focus on the pertinent issues, the meetings have a better than average rate of covering all the ground and finishing on time.

THE MANAGEMENT GUIDES

'Especially for people who have neither the time nor the inclination for ploughing through the normal tomes...'
The Daily Telegraph

Asserting Yourself

Delegating

Handling Stress

Making Time

Managing

Managing Yourself

Motivating

Negotiating

Planning

Running Meetings

Selecting People

Understanding Behaviour

These books are available from your local bookshop or from the publishers:

Oval Books, 335 Kennington Road, London SE11 4QE
Telephone: (0207) 582 7123; Fax: (0207) 582 4887;
E-mail: info@ovalbooks.com